A
CONSERVATIVE
CHRISTIAN
DECLARATION

A
CONSERVATIVE
CHRISTIAN
DECLARATION

—◆—

KEVIN T. BAUDER
SCOTT ANIOL
DAVID DE BRUYN
RYAN J. MARTIN
JASON PARKER
MICHAEL RILEY

RELIGIOUS ✦ AFFECTIONS
— M I N I S T R I E S —
www.religiousaffections.org

A CONSERVATIVE CHRISTIAN DECLARATION

First printing, 2014
Printed in the Unites States of America

Cover design: David Fassett

ISBN-13 978-0-9824582-9-7
ISBN-10 0-9824582-9-0

Table of Contents

Introduction

FULFILLING A DESIRE I've had for some time now, in July 2013 I gathered together a group of pastors and ministry educators to discuss the future of conservative Christianity. As a result of that meeting, we worked for a period of twelve months to formulate a document that would accomplish the following goals:

1. We want to articulate clearly a fully orbed conservative Christianity that includes both doctrine and practice (including holy living and rightly ordered worship).

2. We want to help answer and prevent common caricatures of our positions on these matters.

3. We want a statement that like-minded Christians can rally around as an accurate expression of our convictions, while allowing for appropriate differences among us.

4. We want to produce a statement that can be used as a tool to teach biblical conservatism.

Toward this end, we penned "A Conservative Christian Declaration." We see this document as very similar to statements like the "Chicago Statement on Biblical Inerrancy," the "Danvers Statement on Biblical Manhood and Womanhood," and even recent documents like the T4G Affirmations and Denials and the Gospel Coalition documents. Our

Declaration defines what we believe to be important in a simple way. We also anticipate that it will be used similarly to the documents mentioned. It is a statement that individuals can use to articulate their views or that churches and other institutions can adopt or use as a teaching tool for adult discipleship. Before moving to the declaration, here are a few clarifications and explanations of its underlying purposes:

1. We acknowledge that certain doctrinal commitments that are essential to Christianity are not articulated in the document. This statement does not fully articulate the fundamentals of the Christian faith. We look to the traditional creeds and confessions for that.

2. We do not intend to imply that those who find affinity with the ideas expressed in this document will be able to work together in every circumstance (church planting, church membership, etc.). Doctrinal and practical matters beyond the concerns of this statement (such as denominational distinctives) will and should influence cooperation between Christians.

3. We see this statement as an articulation of ideas that go beyond our core confessions. The Conservative Christian Declaration helps to define certain values

that we consider important across denominational lines and that we fear have been lost in contemporary evangelicalism.

We would affirm as a foundation to this declaration the system of doctrine expressed in the early creeds of Christianity (see the Appendices for the full texts of these historic creeds):

1. The Apostles' Creed
2. The Nicene Creed
3. The Definition of Chalcedon
4. The Athanasian Creed

Furthermore, we would insist upon the affirmation of additional doctrinal clarification and refinement provided by at least one other post-Reformation confession of faith. These might include one of the following (see Appendix E for web sites where you can read the texts of these confessions):

1. The Belgic Confession of Faith
2. The Heidelberg Catechism
3. The Schleitheim Confession
4. The Westminster Confession of Faith
5. The Second London Baptist Confession / The Philadelphia Baptist Confession
6. The Thirty-Nine Articles of the Church of England
7. The New Hampshire Baptist Confession
8. The Baptist Faith and Message

In other words, we believe that the early creeds and at least one post-Reformation confession are necessary for summarizing biblical Christianity today. The Conservative Christian Declaration assumes traditional Christian and evangelical doctrine, adding important distinctives that we believe have been overlooked in recent years.

In the pages that follow, you will find a preamble to the Declaration, followed by articles of affirmation and denial. We then offer brief explanations as clarifications of each article in the Declaration.

The authors of this declaration do not consider it to be the final word on the subjects that it discusses. We recognize that we ourselves are in the process of learning, and we anticipate that both those who agree and those who disagree with this Declaration will help us to arrive at a more complete understanding of the truth. Consequently, both the statement itself and the explanatory chapters may be revised from time to time. While we have published these pages only after considerable thought, and while we are prepared to defend the ideas that we here articulate, we hold ourselves open to challenge and are prepared to be convinced of error and misstatement.

I would like to personally thank the authors who worked together on this document. We can truly say that this is not the work of one man; we have long since lost the points where one person's ideas end and another's begin. We also could not have completed the project without the helpful comments of other friends who read drafts, including Greg Stiekes, Taigen Joos, Deborah Forteza, David Huffstutler, Mike Harding, Mark Snoeberger, T. J. Klapperich, Greg Linscott, Becky Aniol, Mark Ward Jr., and Debbie Bauder. Finally, we are thankful for the beautiful design work provided by David Fassett (cover) and Kevin Mungons (typography) who thoughtfully and accurately captured in their art what we have tried to express in the prose.

Scott Aniol
Fort Worth, Texas

Preamble

In his farewell address to the Ephesian elders, Paul declared that he was "innocent of the blood" of all, because he had not shrunk from delivering to them "the whole counsel of God" (Acts 20:26–27). At its core, conservative Christianity aims to follow Paul's example in successfully transferring the whole counsel of God to the next generation.

Historically, Christians have committed themselves to perpetuating biblical Christianity by pursuing absolute truth, goodness, and beauty. These transcendent realities, which are grounded in the character of God, are expressed through his works and his Word. In every age, Christians have determined to believe God's truth, live out God's goodness, and love God's beauty, preserving these transcendentals by nurturing expressions, forms, and institutions capable of carrying their weight.

More recently, many Christians have abandoned their commitment to these ideals and are therefore failing, in one respect or another, to pursue fully orbed biblical Christianity. The result is a shrunken creed, a waning piety, and a worship that has become irreverent and trivial. We object to this religious reductionism and desire to reclaim the entire heritage of Christian doctrine, obedience, and adoration.

We equally object to those movements attempting to preserve traditions that are not biblical Christianity but rather a progressivism from the past. An innovation is not made less an innovation because of its antiquity. Humanly invented doctrines, objects of piety, and elements of worship will never be part of a truly Christian tradition.

The following declaration reaffirms a historic commitment to fully orbed conservative Christianity. We believe in transcendent, absolute principles of truth, goodness, and beauty; we are confident that such principles are knowable; and we are determined to align ourselves and our ministries to those principles in our pursuit of the whole counsel of God. We also pledge to conserve those institutions and forms that best reflect a recognition of and respect for this transcendent order. Since culture is nurtured within systems of values and is not created in a vacuum, every culture-maker builds upon what has come before. Consequently, we choose to build on those forms that have been nurtured within the community of Christian faith, affirming that they best express the transcendent character and nature of God.

We offer this Declaration out of a deep love for Christ, his gospel, his inerrant Word, and his church, and from a humble desire to help churches conserve and nourish historic, biblical Christianity by affirming the teachings of the Bible concerning truth, goodness, beauty, and rightly ordered affections in life and ministry.

11

Articles of Affirmation and Denial

ARTICLE 1: On the Gospel

We affirm that the gospel of Jesus Christ is the boundary of Christian faith (1 Cor. 15). We also affirm that to ignore this boundary by granting Christian recognition to those who deny the gospel is to demean the gospel itself (2 John 1:10).

We deny that Christian fellowship is possible with those who deny the fundamentals of the gospel, including (among others) the inerrancy of Scripture, the virgin birth, the deity of Christ, his sacrificial atonement, and justification by grace alone through faith alone in Christ alone.

ARTICLE 2: On the Whole Counsel of God

We affirm that the center and apex of Christian faith and fellowship is the whole counsel of God, including right belief, right living, and right affection (Deut. 6:1–9). We further affirm that the transmission of biblical Christianity necessarily involves the preservation and cultivation of the entire system of faith (Acts 20:27).

We deny that belief in the gospel alone is adequate for healthy Christian worship, fellowship, and devotion.

ARTICLE 3: On Transcendentals

We affirm that truth, goodness, and beauty are transcendent realities rooted in the nature of God and ultimately inseparable from each other (Phil. 4:8). Beliefs are true when they correspond to God's understanding; acts are good when they correspond to God's understanding of virtue; objects are beautiful when they are fulfilling their God-intended purpose in a God pleasing way in accordance with their God-given nature. Nevertheless, right beliefs, morals, and affections are not always transparent, and so their relative truth, goodness, and beauty require careful judgment to discern.

We deny that right belief is sufficient to please the Lord. We also deny that truth, morality, or beauty become different things relative to different perceiving subjects (though we grant that humans never perceive in a detached and absolute way). We further deny that right beliefs, morals, and affections are always easy to discern.

ARTICLE 4: On Ordinate Affections

We affirm that Christians can speak meaningfully of orthopathy, or rightly ordered affections and appropriate worship (Deut. 6:5, Matt. 22:37, Heb. 12:28). As the doctrines of the gospel are fundamental to Christianity, so is rightly ordered love for God.

We deny that Christianity is merely assent or commitment to a set of doctrinal propositions that explain the gospel.

ARTICLE 5: On the Appetites

We affirm that manipulation of the visceral appetites is dangerous to rightly ordered worship and Christian piety (Phil. 3:19).

We deny that the transmission of biblical truth can be rightly administered through the use of methods that appeal to the appetites. We further deny that holy affections can be expressed in worship employing aesthetic forms that by design stir the appetites.

ARTICLE 6: On Beauty

We affirm that beauty exists in reality and is to be the pursuit of every believer (Phil. 1:9–11). We also affirm that the recognition of beauty is fundamental to worship and devotion, and a right approach to God entails both a recognition of and a proper response to God's beauty (Ps. 29:2).

We deny that beauty is imposed upon an object by the beholder and that it is nothing more than the beholder's pleasure. We also deny that people of twisted judgments and perceptions can rightly know and love God.

ARTICLE 7: On Scripture-Regulated Worship

We affirm that the worship of God is regulated through his Word. Innovation, however well-intentioned, is "will-worship" (Col. 2:23), violates the free consciences of individual Christians (Rom. 14:5, 23), and is therefore displeasing to God

(Matt. 15:9). We affirm that the circumstances of worship are matters of prudence, informed by the sound judgment that comes through ordinate affection (Prov. 9:10).

We deny that God desires or is pleased by innovation in matters of faith. We deny that silence from God's Word on the circumstances of worship renders them amoral, or their mode of implementation a matter of indifference.

ARTICLE 8: On Works of the Imagination

We affirm that ordinate affections are often expressed and evoked through works of imagination, which function through simile and metaphor. Among these are music, poetry, literature, and other arts. The Word of God itself is a work of imagination. At least two works of imagination are commanded for worship: poetry and music (Col. 3:16).

We deny that God can be known and rightly loved solely through cognition and the intellectual understanding of objective propositional statements about God.

ARTICLE 9: On Harmony and Variety in Ordinate Expression

We affirm that inordinate expressions of worship often arise from hearts that are entangled in disordered loves. We affirm that expressions of orthopathy are grounded in harmony with God's ultimate perception of truth, goodness, and beauty as revealed in Scripture and observed in the created order. We also affirm that the expressions of ordinate love to God have varied between ages and civilizations. We further affirm that these different expressions are nonetheless *equivalent*, representing the same orthopathy.

We deny that inordinate expressions toward God, although

inconsistent with true Christian love, always or necessarily betray inordinate affections. We also deny that harmony with the created order will lead either to complete uniformity of expression, or to a lack of variety. We further deny that the variability of cultural expressions makes these expressions without meaning, and therefore without morality.

ARTICLE 10: On Meaning

We affirm that expressions toward God, be they prayers, preached sermons, poems, or music, may be parsed for their meaning and judged for their appropriateness for worship. We affirm that understanding of meanings is gained both from Scripture and from sources outside Scripture: correct judgments about natural meaning can be made by believers and unbelievers alike (Acts 17:28).

We deny that the subjective nature of these expressions makes it impossible to render a true judgment. We deny that seeking knowledge of meaning outside of Scripture compromises its final authority or denies its sufficiency (Ps. 19, Rom. 1:20ff).

ARTICLE 11: On Popular Culture

We affirm that much of popular culture is formulaic and sentimentalized, and that it tends toward banality and narcissism. We affirm that much popular music, through its stereotyped form, lacks the ability to communicate transcendent truth, virtue, and beauty, which are central to worship. We further affirm that the modes of expression which have emerged from eras shaped largely by the secularizing forces of popular culture are often incompatible with ordinate affection.

16

We deny that a selective rejection of popular culture is tantamount to elitism or a disdain for the average believer. We also deny that there are no contemporary examples of orthopathy, or that orthopathy can be found solely in the past.

ARTICLE 12: On the Cultivation of Christian Tradition

We affirm the importance of beginning our pursuit of sound worship and holy living within the bounds of traditions that we have inherited from the saints of the entire church age (2 Tim. 2:2, Phil. 3:17). Many of these believers, even the ones with whom we would have significant theological disagreements, have had a clearer understanding of what it is to love God rightly than we do. We affirm the value of learning from the culture that developed around and in response to the growth of Christianity.

We deny the chronological snobbery that ignores the past, the naïve longing for some past golden age, and the postmodern inclination to isolate and select elements of historic Christian practice to suit personal taste. We further deny that Christendom represents pure and unmixed Christianity.

ARTICLE 13: On Today's Congregational Music

We affirm that twenty-first-century churches, like the churches of every age, must worship God in their own words, with their own voice. We add the qualification that these expressions must both embody ordinate affection and build on the tradition that represents it, while also answering to the twenty-first-century imagination. We further affirm that all people are to sing with understanding (1 Cor. 14:15) and that good music or poetry may be simple. Finally, we affirm that church music ought to be beautiful.

We deny that musical choices should be made to appease or attract a particular constituency in the church. We deny that the average Christian is capable of appreciating only the simplest kind of music. We deny that good music or poetry worth loving can be shallow, trivial, banal or clichéd. At the same time we also deny that Christians should worship with forms that are incomprehensible to them.

ARTICLE 14: On Our Children

We affirm the necessity of passing these values to our children through regular catechesis, in faithful family worship, and by welcoming all ages into the corporate worship of our churches (Deut. 6:7, Eph. 6:4). Children learn rightly ordered worship and have their imaginations and affections appropriately shaped largely through observation and participation. Thus churches should encourage families to worship together in the corporate gatherings of the church as much as possible or practical.

We deny that the family is more important than or replaces a local church. We further deny that we can adopt a model of children's ministry which aims to entertain our children and still expect them to learn the grace of meaningful worship.

ARTICLE 15: On Local Churches and the Sovereignty of God

We affirm the primacy of the local church in the conservation and nourishment of historic, biblical Christianity. We affirm that godly elders must patiently teach God's Word and model right belief, living, and loving (1 Tim. 3:15, 4:16). We further affirm that such efforts must be fully dependent upon the sovereign will of God, which will ultimately be accomplished (Dan. 4:34–35).

We deny that the transmission of the Christian faith will occur primarily by individuals alone, in families disconnected from local churches, or through parachurch ministries. We further deny that the preservation of Christianity is ultimately dependent upon the meager efforts of finite people and especially any pragmatic methodology or programs.

January 11, 2014

The following pastors and teachers helped to write this document:
Kevin T. Bauder
Scott Aniol
David de Bruyn
Ryan J. Martin
Jason Parker
Michael Riley

ARTICLE 1: On the Gospel

We affirm that the gospel of Jesus Christ is the boundary of Christian faith (1 Cor. 15). We also affirm that to ignore this boundary by granting Christian recognition to those who deny the gospel is to demean the gospel itself (2 John 1:10). *We deny* that Christian fellowship is possible with those who deny the fundamentals of the gospel, including (among others) the inerrancy of Scripture, the virgin birth, the deity of Christ, his sacrificial atonement, and justification by grace alone through faith alone in Christ alone.

—⁓—

Here is found the most fundamental difference
between liberalism and Christianity—
liberalism is altogether in the imperative mood,
while Christianity begins with a triumphant indicative;
liberalism appeals to man's will, while Christianity announces,
first, a gracious act of God.
—J. Gresham Machen, *Christianity and Liberalism*

CHRISTIANITY IS IRREDUCIBLY DOCTRINAL. It is always more than doctrine, but it is never less. The reason that Christianity cannot fail to be doctrinal is that the gospel always involves doctrine. Paul's example bears out this assertion: when he defines the gospel, he appeals to two elements. The first is a sequence of historical events, namely, that Jesus Christ died (the evidence for which is that he was buried), and Jesus Christ rose again (the evidence for which is that he was seen by witnesses). Paul's central argument in 1 Corinthians 15 is that if the historicity of these events is denied, the gospel falls; without them, Christian hope vanishes. Without these events, Christianity cannot exist.

These events, however, are not the whole gospel. Hundreds of criminals suffered the same fate as Jesus of Nazareth. Furthermore, even if the dead body of Jesus were to be revived, that would be merely a novelty of history unless it was theologically interpreted. Paul states the correct interpretation: Jesus died *for our sins in accordance with the Scriptures*. He was raised *on the third day in accordance with the Scriptures*.

These explanations are filled with importance. To say that *Jesus died for our sins* is to affirm that 1) God possesses the authority to say what is sin, 2) we are sinners, 3) sin merits judgment, and 4) there is One qualified to take that judgment in our place. To be qualified to bear our sins, the Bearer must be 1) without sin, 2) like us, and 3) of infinite worth.

Such explanations could continue. What should be clear, however, is that Paul's brief summary of the gospel, which is the essence of the Christian message, is unavoidably doctrinal. To deny the historicity of the events of the gospel is to deny the gospel. To deny the biblical interpretation of those events is also to deny the gospel.

The gospel is what unites Christians. Where the gospel is denied, either explicitly or implicitly, no true fellowship (*koinonia*) exists. To claim to have Christian fellowship with those who deny the gospel is to demean the gospel, to remove it from its rightful place as the boundary of Christian fellowship. Those who demean the gospel ought never be looked to as models of wise Christian living or leadership.

In terms of Christian fellowship, then, our commitment to the gospel always is more central than our commitment to specific worship forms. For example, beautiful worship does not somehow make a denial of justification through faith alone permissible. Some churches have maintained "traditional" worship practices while abandoning the gospel. They are not fitting objects of Christian recognition.

ARTICLE 2:
On the Whole Counsel of God

We affirm that the center and apex of Christian faith and fellowship is the whole counsel of God, including right belief, right living, and right affection (Deut. 6:1–9). We further affirm that the transmission of biblical Christianity necessarily involves the preservation and cultivation of the entire system of faith (Acts 20:27). —ᴟ— *We deny* that belief in the gospel alone is adequate for healthy Christian worship, fellowship, and devotion.

—ᴟ—

THE GOSPEL FORMS the boundary of Christian fellowship: outside the gospel, no Christianity and no Christian fellowship can exist. Those who agree on the gospel, however, still disagree about many issues. Some of these issues are relatively trivial (for instance, the identity of the "sons of God" in Genesis 6); others have greater importance.

About these issues, we affirm that two ditches must be avoided. On one side are those who raise every issue to the level of the gospel. Disagreements on secondary matters (such as views of the ordering of events during the end times) are made tests of Christian fellowship. This kind of "everythingism" diminishes the importance of the gospel. It writes everything in characters that are bold and uppercase; by emphasizing everything, it emphasizes nothing. Consequently, the "weightier matters of the law," the "first and greatest commandment" is brought down to the level of the least important matters.

On the other side are those who grasp the central importance of the gospel and therefore insist that all else is inconsequential. In such cases, views of baptism and the Table, church order (including polity, membership, and discipline), eschatology, and many other doctrines and practices are minimized. We wish to push back against such essentialism: these "secondary" doctrines and practices, while not always necessary to the being of the church, are of vital importance to its well-being.

We contend that "gospel minimalism" harms churches, not because of what it emphasizes, but because of what it neglects. Therefore, while affirming the place of the gospel as the boundary of fellowship, we insist that the whole counsel of God is the center of fellowship, and that pursuit of this center is of irreplaceable value for worship, fellowship, and devotion. Furthermore, this center is not merely doctrinal. It includes elements of orthodoxy, orthopraxy, and orthopathy.

ARTICLE 3: On Transcendentals

We affirm that truth, goodness, and beauty are transcendent realities rooted in the nature of God and ultimately inseparable from each other (Phil. 4:8). Beliefs are true when they correspond to God's understanding; acts are good when they correspond to God's understanding of virtue; objects are beautiful when they are fulfilling their God-intended purpose in a God pleasing way in accordance with their God-given nature. Nevertheless, right beliefs, morals, and affections are not always transparent, and so their relative truth, goodness, and beauty require careful judgment to discern. —— *We deny* that right belief is sufficient to please the Lord. We also deny that truth, morality, or beauty become different things relative to different perceiving subjects (though we grant that humans never perceive in a detached and absolute way). We further deny that right beliefs, morals, and affections are always easy to discern.

—

BELIEF IN TRANSCENDENT TRUTH, goodness, and beauty is rooted in a recognition that God is the source, sustainer, and end of all things. Romans 11:36 declares that "from him and through him and to him are all things." The Bible clearly proclaims that God is self-existent and self-sustaining, that all things come from him. All truth is grounded in the reality that God is True. All virtue is grounded in the reality that God is Good. All beauty is grounded in the reality that God is Beautiful. Brute facts apart from God do not and never can exist; such facts are what they are because God ordains them to be so. No genuinely moral standards can merely be conceived by convention apart from God. Rather, actions are moral or immoral because of their conformity (or lack thereof) to God's character. Beauty does not merely exist in the eye of the beholder, though certainly the beholder can perceive what is beautiful. Rather, things are beautiful when they are doing what God meant them to do as God meant them to do it.

With these considerations in mind, Christians as image-bearers of God must commit themselves to thinking God's thoughts after him, to behaving in ways that conform to God's moral perfection, and to loving those things that God calls lovely.

The recognition of truth, goodness, and beauty is implicit in Philippians 4:8, which articulates tests by which Christians may judge the real value of all things.

> Finally, brothers, whatever is true, whatever is honorable, whatever is just, whatever is pure, whatever is lovely, whatever is commendable, if there is any excellence, if there is anything worthy of praise, think about these things.

Since God is the source, sustainer, and end of all things, a conservative Christian believes in real and transcendent standards of truth, goodness, and beauty.

ARTICLE 4: On Ordinate Affections

We affirm that Christians can speak meaningfully of orthopathy, or rightly ordered affections and appropriate worship (Deut. 6:5, Matt. 22:37, Heb. 12:28). As the doctrines of the gospel are fundamental to Christianity, so is rightly ordered love for God. —⁓— *We deny* that Christianity is merely assent or commitment to a set of doctrinal propositions that explain the gospel.

—⁓—

PART OF THE IMAGE OF GOD in humanity is the capacity to love, for God loves and he is love. Love is a function of the will, and not merely of the understanding. A right relationship to God involves more than an abstract or theoretical understanding of the truth of his Word. Rather, it includes grasping the truths of God's perfections and mighty deeds and relishing these truths as beautiful and lovely.

The Scriptures clearly teach that the most important human duty is to love God. Moses commanded the people of Israel, "Hear, O Israel: The Lord our God, the Lord is one. You shall love the Lord your God with all your heart and with all your soul and with all your might" (Deut. 6:4–5). Jesus repeated this great Shema when he answered the lawyer's question concerning the greatest commandment: "Hear, O Israel! The Lord our God, the Lord is one. And you shall love the Lord your God with all your heart and with all your soul and with all your mind and with all your strength" (Mark 12:29–30). By loving God in this way, we fulfill the great end for which God made us.

The greatest commandment at once demands not just love, but a certain kind of love over against other kinds of love. For instance, true love of God must engage every capacity of our personhood: heart, soul, mind, and strength. Furthermore, it must engage these capacities to their utmost: we must love God with *all* of our heart, soul, mind, and strength. The duty of loving God rightly, however, implies the possibility of loving him wrongly, and that possibility raises the problem of orthopathy, or rightly ordered loves (or, more broadly, affections).

At its core, orthopathy is divine love—love born in us by the Spirit of God. No one can love God without loving his Son Jesus Christ, and this love of God in Christ comes only through the inner work of the Holy Spirit (2 Cor. 13:14; cf. 1 Cor. 2:14–16). No one can love God without being made new, without being "born from above" by the Spirit of God. In John 1:12–13, those who receive and believe Jesus Christ are the same ones who are "born . . . of God." The fruit of the Spirit is love (Gal. 5:22; cf. Col. 1:8; 2 Tim. 1:7). The Holy Spirit pours God's love into the believer's heart (Rom. 5:5). We love God and the people God loves because of the indwelling Spirit of God (1 John 4:16, 19). Those who do not love Christ fall under a curse (1 Cor. 16:22). The call to love God rightly is first and foremost a call to confess that Jesus Christ is Lord to the glory of God the Father. Those who have so believed the gospel ought then to order rightly their love for God and to worship him appropriately through Jesus Christ.

Human beings love all sorts of things, and we order our loves sometimes intentionally, sometimes unintentionally. It would be silly for a father to love his pet dog more than his daughters. Similarly, it would be abhorrent if that man treated his daughters like he does his dog. By either wrongly exaggerating his love for the animal or by wrongly diminishing his love for his daughters, he would be doing wrong by feeling wrongly. The appropriate expression of loves for different things is shaped by the natural use of those things. One salivates over food, laughs at jokes, takes in a sunset, kisses one's wife. Paul does not bid husbands to love their wives any way they wish, but rather just as Christ loved the church.

Likewise, love for God ought to have a different shape or contour from the things that people love in this world. Consequently, the author of Hebrews bids us to "offer to God acceptable worship, with reverence and awe." This kind of worship befits a God who is, who has always been, and who always will be, "a consuming fire" (Heb. 12:28–29). Worship for God, by which our love for God is outwardly expressed, ought to be shaped by the object of our worship. Appropriate worship should never be offered in confusion and disorder, but in wisdom, peace, and harmony (1 Cor. 14:23, 33, 40). Paul likewise stressed the necessity of orthopathy when he concluded his letter to the Ephesians: "Grace be with all who love our Lord Jesus Christ with love incorruptible" (Eph. 6:24).

One kind of love for Christ is earthward and worldly, and it will die with the world that is perishing. Another kind of love for Christ is heavenward and incorruptible, just as the Lord that is its object. Christians ought to be people who have "reverence for Christ" (Eph. 5:21). While even our best worship in this life finds acceptance only when offered in the name of Christ and bathed in the blood of the Lamb, the church must nevertheless call up all her powers to "become what she is," worshiping in accordance with the reality that the Spirit of God indwells her (1 Cor. 3:2–4; 16–17; 5:7–8).

ARTICLE 5: On the Appetites

We affirm that manipulation of the visceral appetites is dangerous to rightly ordered worship and Christian piety (Phil. 3:19). —∾— *We deny* that the transmission of biblical truth can be rightly administered through the use of methods that appeal to the appetites. We further deny that holy affections can be expressed in worship employing aesthetic forms that by design stir the appetites.

—∾—

WE BELIEVE THAT GOD created humanity to consist of inner and outer, or body and a soul, and that these are so connected as to influence each other. Christian theologians before the modern era generally believed that inner and outer humanity each produced distinct desires, the higher corresponding to the will of the soul, and that these desires were called the *affections* (Col. 3:1–4). The lower desires, which corresponded to the body, were called the *passions* (1 Cor. 7:9; Phil. 3:19). The Bible does not teach that the desires of the body are necessarily evil (John 19:28) or that the desires of the soul are necessarily good (e.g., 1 Cor. 3:3). Nevertheless, inner humanity (the soul) is recognized as the seat of religion (John 4:23–24).

When we speak of the passions or "visceral appetites," we are referring to innate impulses created by God in humans to preserve health and welfare. God gave people these impulses because the things that the body desires, such as food, drink, and sleep, are necessary to live. Even though they are necessary, however, the Bible condemns an inordinate attachment to these appetites. Paul speaks, in Philippians 3, of those who "walk as enemies of the cross of Christ." He explains in verse 19, "Their end is destruction, their God is their belly, and they glory in their shame, with minds set on earthly things." Paul certainly has corporeal needs in view when he says in 1 Corinthians 9:27: "But I discipline my body and keep it under control, lest after preaching to others I myself should be disqualified." Because the things of this world are passing away, they do not deserve unrestricted devotion. God expects believers to keep bodily appetites under control (Gal. 5:16–24; Eph. 5:3–20; Phil. 3:20–21; 1 Peter 4:3–5; 2 Peter 1:3–4; 2:17–22).

This biblical testimony explains why we object when religious appeals are directed to the visceral appetites. These appetites are easily abused, especially by the unregenerate. Since we are embodied beings, the bodily appetites are often much more attractive to our senses and consequently much more powerful over us. Most people desire immediate pleasure over delayed gratification, bodily satisfaction over spiritual consideration, and self-indulgence over self-control. For example, our embodied existence leads us to give ourselves to leisurely diversion more readily than to sermons that require thought and attentiveness.

Some Christian leaders try to attract people to hear God's Word or to enjoy other spiritual pleasures by promising them the satisfaction of these more immediate, sensual desires. This kind of tactic is dishonest and genuinely sinister. What it arouses is the very thing that Christ's Lordship requires us to mortify in following him. The pleasures that Christians offer the world are first and foremost spiritual, unseen, and (in a proper sense) rational.

Attempts to minister through methods that appeal to the appetites are akin to the "eloquence" that Paul refused to employ when he preached the gospel (1 Cor. 1–2). Paul clearly denounced any such ministry because it would empty Christ's cross of its power (1 Cor. 1:17). This kind of ministry is "doomed to pass away" (1 Cor. 2:6). Unsaved humans do not receive the things of the Spirit of God because they do not have the Spirit, and the Spirit's teachings (see 1 Cor. 2:6–10) are only understood by those who have received the Spirit (1 Cor. 2:12–14). Ministries that try to make the gospel attractive by exciting visceral appetites are in effect attempting to circumvent the necessary role of the Spirit of God. Believers who want to place the power of the gospel on display and who hope to ensure that professed faith rests in the power of God rather than in human wisdom will preach Christ without such appeals (1 Cor. 2:5).

While we recognize that worship in this life engages the body, we insist that true worship cannot be offered in an overtly earthly, sensual way. Because God is Spirit, the higher, holy affections of believers in worship are not carried appropriately by aesthetic forms that are designed to reflect and manipulate visceral appetites. Indeed, as Christians, we are explicitly given this command: "Finally, brothers, whatever is true, whatever is honorable, whatever is just, whatever is pure, whatever is lovely, whatever is commendable, if there is any excellence, if there is anything worthy of praise, think about these things" (Phil. 4:8). So may we live, so may we minister, and so may we worship.

ARTICLE 6: On Beauty

We affirm that beauty exists in reality and is to be the pursuit of every believer (Phil. 1:9–11). We also affirm that the recognition of beauty is fundamental to worship and devotion, and a right approach to God entails both a recognition of and a proper response to God's beauty (Ps. 29:2). —⁓— *We deny* that beauty is imposed upon an object by the beholder and that it is nothing more than the beholder's pleasure. We also deny that people of twisted judgments and perceptions can rightly know and love God.

—⁓—

ALTHOUGH MOST CONSERVATIVE evangelicals affirm the reality of transcendent, absolute truth and goodness, some deny that beauty really exists apart from the enjoyment of the one who perceives it. Instead, they maintain that beauty is only "in the eye of the beholder" and is purely relative.

On the contrary, we strongly affirm that beauty is transcendent and real for at least four reasons:

First, the self-existence of God demands the reality of genuine beauty outside of and above the created order (John 17:5, 24; Rev. 4:11). Like truth and morality, beauty finds its source in the nature and character of God. Consequently, objects may be rightly called beautiful, not simply because a human delights in them, but because they reflect Supreme Beauty.

Second, Scripture speaks of God's own beauty (2 Chron. 20:21; Job 40:9–10; Ps. 9:8, 27:4, 45:2–4, 104:1, 145:10–12, Isa. 42:14, Zech. 9:17). God's glory is his beauty. This observation further indicates that God is the ultimate standard by which beauty must be judged.

Third, God has declared particular things to be beautiful. He called his new creation beautiful (Gen. 1:4, 10, 12, 18, 21, and 25). He prescribed specific artistic instructions for liturgical adornments so that they would manifest "glory and beauty" (Ex. 28:2). Such affirmations strongly imply the reality of a transcendent standard by which beauty must be judged.

Fourth, God requires his people to delight in things that are genuinely beautiful. For example, Philippians 4:8 commands believers to "think on" things that are "lovely" (literally "towards affection"), "commendable" (admirable), and "worthy of praise." These terms are each closely connected to a right understanding of beauty, and they imply that some objects are worthy and others unworthy of delight.

39

Beauty is real. Christians should delight themselves only in those things that are worthy of enjoyment. Scripture explicitly declares some things to be worthy of such pleasure, and what determines their worthiness is conformity to the beauty of God himself.

Because many people believe beauty to consist in personal delight, they infer that it is merely relative. They further infer that discussions of beauty are incidental and unimportant. To the contrary, we affirm that beauty is real, that it is rooted in God himself, and that we are responsible to discern diligently what is worthy of delight. We affirm these propositions for three reasons.

First, nothing is worthy of delight except whatever reflects God's own enjoyment. Delighting in that which offends God is sin. Enjoyment of the ugly (as God determines ugliness) is to fall short of the glory of God (Rom. 3:23).

Second, in rightly ordered worship we ascribe beauty to God and worship him in "holy beauty" (Ps. 29:2). The essence of praise is delight in the absolute beauty of God. The heart of true worship, including corporate worship, is to magnify the beautiful glory of God.

Third, when people delight in ugliness, their judgments and perceptions become twisted. They can no longer truly apprehend and appreciate the absolute beauty of God (Rom. 1:23–25). Without a transcendent reference point, they even become capable of fastening their affections upon activities that violate the natural order.

The right appreciation of beauty requires humility. All who wish to delight in the genuinely beautiful must submit to a standard that exists outside of and above themselves. For fallen human beings, this necessary submission poses three problems.

First, we often fail to perceive real beauty because sin casts a shroud of ugliness over it. Sin so scars the visage of creation that we often fail to detect the traces of the beauty that God has fashioned. Because God intends to redeem fallen creation, he will bring great glory out of much that is now grotesque. He will reshape and restore what sin has damaged. We do not yet see things as they will be, and with our sight so dimmed we must distinguish the damage that sin has caused (which truly is ugly) from the created thing that has been damaged. If we fail to mark this distinction, we shall mistake beauty for ugliness.

Second, and conversely, we may mistake ugliness for beauty. In the absence of a transcendent reference point we tend to define beauty in terms of utility. In particular, we mistake the gratification of our appetites for beauty. Thus confused, we become capable of misappropriating genuinely beautiful objects for uses that are hideous. We subject the beautiful to our appetites in ways that reflect our rebellion against God. Such uses of beauty are desecrations. They can be avoided only by disciplining ourselves away from the unreflective gratification of our appetites and humbly seeking out the reality of true beauty.

Third, while we acknowledge a transcendent and perfect standard of beauty, we recognize that no fallen human has ever fully understood or appropriated this standard. We know in part and we see in part. Consequently, each person and each culture perceives only a part of what is truly beautiful. Furthermore, while their knowledge of the beautiful will certainly overlap, each person and each culture perceives a somewhat different part. For this reason, no one individual and no one culture should be ceded the absolute right to say what is beautiful and what is not. One of the most useful tasks that Christians can perform is criticism (in the proper sense of the term) that aims for understanding, opening themselves to the possibility of seeing the genuine beauty that someone else perceives.

In summary, we should take aesthetic pleasure only in those things that are truly beautiful—truly *worthy* of delight—as compared to the absolute standard of God's beauty and glory. To do otherwise is sin, and to regularly pursue pleasure in what is ugly hinders ordinate worship and praise to God.

Article 7:
On Scripture Regulated Worship

We affirm that the worship of God is regulated through his Word. Innovation, however well-intentioned, is "will-worship" (Col. 2:23), violates the free consciences of individual Christians (Rom. 14:5, 23), and is therefore displeasing to God (Matt. 15:9). We affirm that the circumstances of worship are matters of prudence, informed by the sound judgment that comes through ordinate affection (Prov. 9:10). — *We deny* that God desires or is pleased by innovation in matters of faith. We deny that silence from God's Word on the circumstances of worship renders them amoral, or their mode of implementation a matter of indifference.

—⁓—

THE CHRISTIAN CHURCH is founded upon the teachings of the Lord Jesus Christ (Matt. 17:1–8; 28:18). Jesus has purchased the church with his own blood, and he owns it absolutely (Acts 20:28; 1 Cor. 3:11, 23). He gave himself for it that he might present it to himself, holy and without blemish (Eph. 5:27). He appointed his apostles and prophets to speak his words to his followers as he revealed them by his Holy Spirit (Matt. 28:19; Acts 1:21–22; 1 Cor. 2:10, 13). Since the apostles and prophets are no longer living, Christians esteem their writings, canonized in the New Testament, as the authoritative teaching of Christ himself (Matt. 10:40; John 13:13–15, 20; Acts 1:2; 1 Cor. 15:3; 1 Thess. 2:13). Since they communicated the word of Christ, the apostles and prophets serve as the foundation of the church (Eph. 2:19–22; Eph. 4:11–16; 1 Cor. 12:28; cf. Matt. 16:18; Rev. 21:14). Their teachings are fully authoritative, as from Christ himself. Consequently, Paul told believers to hold fast to the apostolic tradition (1 Cor. 11:2; 2 Thess. 2:15; 1 Cor. 15:1–3), for this tradition comes from Christ. Paul further commanded the Corinthian church, "Be imitators of me, as I am of Christ" (1 Cor. 11:1). This doctrinal foundation, given to Christ's apostles, is the "good deposit" of apostolic teaching that Timothy was to guard (1 Tim. 6:20; cf. 2 Tim. 1:14; Jude 20). Although apostles could commit personal errors (Gal. 2:11–14), disobedience to an apostle's commands—i.e., disobedience to apostolic Scripture—constitutes disobedience to Christ himself (2 Thess. 3:14–15).

This robust understanding of the authority of the Word of God leads us to assert that Christian churches must worship God in ways that are prescribed and regulated by God through Christ's apostles. Since Christ alone has authority over the church, he has the right to say how we must worship. Any attempt to innovate, whether in doctrine or in forms of worship, constitutes a usurpation of the authority of Christ.

The apostle Paul observed that some in Colossae were inventing new doctrines, regulations, and forms of worship that had not been authorized by Christ through his apostles (Col. 2:16–22). Paul designated these innovations as *etheolothreskia*, a term that means *will worship* (KJV) or *self-made religion* (ESV). He made it clear that this kind of roll-your-own-at-home religion was a form of idolatry. In other words, the faith that Christians profess is not self-made. God has revealed it. As he has prescribed our doctrine, God has prescribed our worship.

By attending to New Testament commands and practices, we can ascertain which activities or elements of worship God wishes a church to employ.

Exalting God through the proclamation of his word was commanded by Christ, by Paul, and by Peter (Matt. 28:20; 2 Tim. 4:2–5; 1 Peter 4:11). Such preaching was actually heard in the assemblies of early Christian churches (Acts 6:2; 14:7, 21–22; 15:35; 18:24, 27; 20:7–9, 26–32; cf. 1 Cor. 1:17; Eph. 4:11ff; Col. 3:16; 1 Tim. 4:13). We regard biblical preaching as a required element of worship.

The apostle Paul directly commanded the public reading of Scripture in the churches (1 Tim. 4:13; cf. Col. 4:16; 1 Thess. 5:27). As the historical record shows, the reading of Scripture was a regular practice of the apostolic churches. We regard the reading of the biblical text as an prescribed element of corporate worship.

Public prayer was both commanded and practiced (Acts 1:14, 24; 2:42; 3:1; 4:31; 6:4; 12:5; 13:3; 16:25; 20:36; etc.; 1 Cor. 11:4–5; 14:15–16; Eph. 6:18; Phil. 4:6; Col. 4:2; 1 Thess. 5:17; James 5:13; etc.). One way that the church prayed was by singing to God (1 Cor. 14:15). Furthermore, the apostolic churches were specifically commanded to sing (Col. 3:16; Eph. 5:17–20; James 5:13; cf. 1 Cor. 14:26). We regard both prayer and singing as necessary elements of corporate worship.

Sometimes the early church accompanied its prayer with fasting (Acts 13:1–3; 14:23; cf. Matt. 9:15). While fasting was never specifically commanded of New Testament churches, it was clearly practiced.

The apostolic churches regularly practiced giving. Paul referred to the monetary support churches gave their spiritual leaders as an "offering," a term that carries distinct liturgical overtones (Phil. 4:18). Paul further commanded churches to care for needy believers, and to take up the collections for them when they were gathered (1 Cor. 16:1–4). We regard regular giving as a necessary element of corporate worship.

Jesus himself commanded Christian churches to partake in the Lord's Supper, and this command was elaborated by the apostle Paul (1 Cor. 11:23–26). Jesus and his apostles also commanded believers to be baptized (Matt. 28:19; Acts 2:38; 22:16; Rom. 6:1–4). Baptism is also an act of worship, not only for the person baptized, but also for those who, while observing it, are reminded of the work and perfections of God represented in that holy sign of the profession of our faith. Both baptism and the Lord's Table were widely practiced in the churches of the New Testament. We regard these ordinances as indispensable elements of corporate worship.

47

The New Testament provides the authoritative pattern for worship. To introduce some other element is to ask Christians to go beyond what the apostles have given them authority to do (Matt. 15:9). Consequently, adding other practices besides those that are revealed in the New Testament violates the consciences of sincere Christians whose souls are bound to their Lord as Master (Rom. 14:5, 23). We urge those who so desire to add elements to their worship that Christ has not prescribed to consider carefully what is at stake. They may be building with combustible materials or, even worse, doing damage to Christ's temple (1 Cor. 3:10–17).

Nevertheless, we do not believe that following the apostolic pattern requires us to do exactly what they did in exactly the way they did it. The New Testament prescribes the elements of worship, but it does not always specify the circumstances by which those elements are to be implemented. For example, the New Testament does not require Christians to use a specific language, to gather under specific lighting, to amplify their voices through specific architecture or other technologies, or to order their services in a specific sequence (though we are commanded that our services be done decently and in order (1 Cor. 14:40).

In other words, while Christians are told *what* they may do in worship, they are not always told exactly *how* they are to do it. We recognize that churches exercise liberty in their choice of these circumstances. Nevertheless many (often overlooked) biblical teachings do provide principles for worshipping God with the prescribed elements. Therefore, while the choice of circumstances is a matter of prudence, it is not a matter of indifference. The fact that circumstances are not prescribed does not make them amoral or indifferent. The worship of the true and living God is the principal business of all Christians, and they must exercise discernment in how they go about this business. Christian leaders above all must choose carefully and wisely how to apply these passages, leading their churches to worship the true and living God (Prov. 9:10).

Furthermore, the fact that the elements of worship are prescribed in Scripture does not imply that every element must be present in every act of corporate worship. For example, baptisms may not occur in every worship service. Some services may appropriately focus on only some of the elements. The overall worship of the church, however, must incorporate all of those elements and only those elements that are prescribed by the New Testament if that worship is to be genuinely biblical.

ARTICLE 8:
On Works of the Imagination

We affirm that ordinate affections are often expressed and evoked through works of imagination, which function through simile and metaphor. Among these are music, poetry, literature, and other arts. The Word of God itself is a work of imagination. At least two works of imagination are commanded for worship: poetry and music (Col. 3:16). —⁓— *We deny* that God can be known and rightly loved solely through cognition and the intellectual understanding of objective propositional statements about God.

—⁓—

WE HOLD THAT WORKS of the imagination (the arts) are more than enjoyable distractions. Nevertheless, many Christians assume that only their cognitive beliefs about God are important, while musical or poetic expressions about God have little purpose beyond making truth about God interesting, enjoyable, or exciting. This attitude leads to the conclusion that the choice to expose one's self to certain works of imagination is merely a matter of preference. Some suggest that the only mark of successful sacred art is whether it ignites "passion" for God.

To reiterate, we hold that works of imagination are more than merely enjoyable diversions. We recognize that this proposition is disputed. In support of it, we offer the following considerations.

First, as we have already argued in Article 4, right affections are central to biblical Christianity. Some affections are appropriate for expression to God, while others are not. The major categories of affection (e.g., love, joy, awe, fear) each include multiple nuances of response, only some of which can rightly be addressed to the Lord. For example, it would be wrong to love God as a parent loves a child, as a biker loves a motorcycle, or as a glutton loves a plate of spaghetti.

Second, right affections are nurtured and cultivated through the imagination. Imagination is that faculty through which the facts and experiences of the world are construed and interpreted, and through which they find their significance. For example, a farmer who is enduring a drought construes a rainy day as a blessing. He welcomes it and responds with joy and gratitude. A fidgety child who wishes to play outdoors construes the same rainy day as an obstruction and a nuisance. She responds with disappointment and perhaps petulance. How the farmer and child imagine the rain shapes their response to it, and their response leads to the expression of different affections.

The same principle is at work in those affections that Christians express toward God. How we imagine God will produce different affections, and different expressions of affection, toward him. Whether one imagines God to be a cruel despot, a warm lover, or a gracious sovereign will affect the kind of response that one feels and articulates toward God.

Third, the goal of the arts—including music and poetry, the arts employed in worship—is to shape and furnish the imagination. These arts (including poetry and music) always go beyond the expression of propositional content. They also express a point of view, a particular imaginative construal of the propositional content, the goal of which is to enable the singer or listener to grasp the perspective of the artist toward the subject. In other words, poetry and music communicate more than propositional content, and this communication is accomplished through the poet's selection of metaphors and other devices, and through the moods and sensibilities expressed by the music.

When these arts have truth about God for their content, they express specific perceptions of God in ways that are designed to shape the imagination. Such matters as the metaphors that are chosen to represent God, the poetic meter, the melodic contour, the rhythm, harmony, form, timbre, and so forth express ways of imagining God and elicit particular responses. These arts can be employed in such a way that the productions represent God as a despot, a lover, or a sovereign—producing the corresponding responses.

Fourth, Scripture itself uses imaginative devices to shape

our vision of reality. The Holy Spirit of God chose particular literary genres, forms, metaphors, and other imaginative devices to communicate truth in Scripture. These choices enable us to imagine reality in a way that corresponds to God's own sovereign understanding. Working in this way, the imaginative content of Scripture also provides both guidelines and limits for new art that is produced today.

Finally, since works of art shape the imagination, and since these imaginative works express and evoke affections, works of art ought to be employed as expressions of right affection. Specifically, Scripture commands that Christians express certain classes of affections toward the Lord. Imaginative works have the power to express those affections, and are fitting and necessary ways in which God can be adored, praised, worshiped, and glorified. Nevertheless, art that imagines God wrongly or provokes inordinate affection toward him must be rejected.

In summary, Scripture commands that truth about God be expressed through works of imagination (Col. 3:16). The purpose of this command is not simply to make God's truth more amusing. Since wrong imaginative expressions can elicit inordinate responses toward God, Christians are responsible both to produce and to choose imaginative expressions that are aesthetically true, i.e., that evoke responses corresponding to the reality of who God is. If we wish to imagine God rightly, not only must our doctrines be propositionally true, but our responses must also be aesthetically true.

ARTICLE 9: On Harmony and Variety in Ordinate Expression

We affirm that inordinate expressions of worship often arise from hearts that are entangled in disordered loves. We affirm that expressions of orthopathy are grounded in harmony with God's ultimate perception of truth, goodness, and beauty as revealed in Scripture and observed in the created order. We also affirm that the expressions of ordinate love to God have varied between ages and civilizations. We further affirm that these different expressions are nonetheless *equivalent*, representing the same orthopathy. —⁓— *We deny* that inordinate expressions toward God, although inconsistent with true Christian love, always or necessarily betray inordinate affections. We also deny that harmony with the created order will lead either to complete uniformity of expression, or to a lack of variety. We further deny that the variability of cultural expressions makes these expressions without meaning, and therefore without morality.

—⁓—

PREFERENCE is a favorite word in debates about worship. It is deployed as an alkali to neutralize the acidity of sharp critiques against particular expressions of worship. Often, *preference* is used to suggest that no absolute value can be assigned to expressions of worship, that we can only evaluate how much one person prefers one expression over another, or that we can only compare one person's preferences to another person's preferences. In the end, this emphasis upon *preference* leads to the conclusion that critics are moralizing over inconsequential matters of taste.

We disagree with this conclusion, though we certainly affirm that believers may prefer one poem or musical composition over another. Within the range of what pleases God, believers may have their favorites. Nevertheless, we deny that the worship wars are childish or short-sighted disputes over the liturgical equivalent of one's taste in ice cream. Our belief is based upon a conviction that art, which is a principal *techne* of worship, is grounded in realities that transcend the created order. Truth, goodness, and beauty, while present in creation, are also above and anterior to it. When humans arrange the raw materials of creation, be they sand and cement for architecture, syllables for poems, or sounds for music, the result has the power either to explain or to distort God's intended order.

When distortion occurs, it often arises from hearts that are disordered in their loves. Romans 1 describes the process by which humanity has elevated creation above the Creator, thereby dooming itself to folly. From the foolishness of that disordered relationship come further activities that reveal the now-depraved human heart. We readily grant that some distortions may not arise from a deliberate intent to falsify or desecrate, but distortions remain distortions in spite of the intentions that give rise to them.

This focus on ordinate expression is not a covert attempt to absolutize the music, poetry, or other expressions of some past era or culture. We deny that those who argue for intrinsic beauty are doomed to a narrow selection of art or that they are characterized by a demand for uniformity in worship expressions. Most of all, we deny that the recognition of ordinate expression constitutes an attempt to enforce our preference upon others.

We affirm that God's variegated creation provides an endless variety of beautiful expressions of worship. Delightful, artistic expressions or ordinate worship (i.e., expressions in harmony with transcendent truth, goodness, and beauty as manifested in God's good creation) can, in principle, be developed in any society where common grace is present. Where special grace is also present, the possibility of such delights abounds yet more. We understand that different expressions will arise across time and geographical space. We do not expect that reverent joy will look and sound the same in African civilizations as it does in European ones, even if both develop under the gospel. We do not expect trembling admiration to look and sound precisely the same to us as it did to Augustine. Nevertheless, we expect that ordinate expressions will be equivalent, though the forms of expression may be unfamiliar.

On the other hand, this delightful variety must not be exploited as a rationale for aesthetic agnosticism. Both ordinate and inordinate expressions exist in great variety. Truth can be communicated in hundreds of languages, but so can lies.

The scene in Revelation 5:9 brings joy to us because of its obvious meaning: God delights to redeem all peoples. Nevertheless, God's delight in many nations is not a biblical sanction for multiculturalism, the teaching that regards all cultural expressions as equal in value (and therefore eliminates the need for both criticism and discernment). Our evaluation of expressions of worship must concede nothing either to a false multiculturalism or to a cultural imperialism. Rather, the expressions of every place and era must be tested for their harmony with transcendent reality and with God's created order.

ARTICLE 10: On Meaning

We affirm that expressions toward God, be they prayers, preached sermons, poems, or music, may be parsed for their meaning and judged for their appropriateness for worship. We affirm that understanding of meanings is gained both from Scripture and from sources outside Scripture: correct judgments about natural meaning can be made by believers and unbelievers alike (Acts 17:28). — *We deny* that the subjective nature of these expressions makes it impossible to render a true judgment. We deny that seeking knowledge of meaning outside of Scripture compromises its final authority or denies its sufficiency (Ps. 19, Rom. 1:20ff).

All things were made through him, and without him
was not any thing made that was made (John 1:3).

For by him all things were created, in heaven and on earth,
visible and invisible, whether thrones or dominions or rulers or
authorities—all things were created through him and for him.
And he is before all things, and in him all things hold together
(Col. 1:16–17).

CHRISTIANS BELIEVE that God created all things. This belief implies several important truths. First, since God created all things, his good creation constitutes an expression of himself. Furthermore, God created nothing without a purpose. His ultimate purpose was to glorify himself, using the things he made to reveal his nature and character. In a very real sense, creation is a revelation of God.

Thus, all creation *means* something. It means what God intended it to mean. It declares his glory and proclaims his handiwork, revealing knowledge of him (Ps. 19:1–2). It clearly presents his invisible attributes, namely, his eternal power and divine nature (Rom. 1:20).

God's creation *means* these things whether or not people acknowledge their meaning. In fact, Paul explains in Romans 1 that unbelievers have suppressed the knowledge of God, even though it is clearly expressed to them through what he has made. That is why they are without excuse.

Another implication of our belief in divine creation is that, since we are made in the image of God, we also have the ability to create. Unlike God, we cannot make something from nothing; we must begin with the material he has made. Like God's creation, however, whatever we create expresses or reveals ourselves, our values, our goals, our delights, and our ambitions.

In other words, all human creations also *mean* something. Consequently, nothing that exists lacks meaning. Everything that we encounter was made either by God or by humans. As with God's creation, so with human creations: the meanings exist whether or not people understand or even acknowledge them.

Meaning is expressed in both content and form. Content is *what* is expressed; form is *how* the content is expressed. Both carry meaning at one or more levels. For example, some meaning is purely stipulative, while other meanings arise through association. These meanings are most flexible. They can change from person to person and may even be idiosyncratic. An example of a divinely stipulated meaning is the association of the rainbow with God's promise never again to destroy the earth with water. An example of a humanly stipulated meaning is the association of the rainbow with homosexuality.

Other meaning is conventional, taught and learned as part of the stuff of life. Conventional meanings are often so habitual as to seem nearly transparent. For example, the United States and Canada employ the convention of driving on the right side of the road. Americans and Canadians often experience disorientation while adapting to the opposite custom in the United Kingdom. Also, many aspects of language function conventionally—if all language were purely stipulative, communication would not be possible.

Still other meaning is natural and intuitive. Evidence that natural meaning exists and is universal can be found in at least two considerations, each of which points to a world of shared meaning. First, whatever God created is expressive because it reveals him, and thus is universal in its message. Layers of stipulative, associative, or conventional meaning may be added on top of the natural meanings of created things, but at some level all humans experience the meaning of created things as pointers to God and his purpose.

Second, universal meaning is possible because people share a common humanity. Because of shared biology, anatomy, and sensibilities, all people experience reality and express themselves in similar ways. Whatever expressions of meaning flow from this shared humanity will be universal and intuitive. Consequently, Christians should be committed not only to interpreting what God intends by his creation, but also what humans intend by the expressions they produce.

Understanding meaning is especially important when these two worlds of meaning intersect, for humans are responsible to speak rightly both to and about God. We must attend to meaning when we read and preach God's written Revelation, when we express ourselves to God through prayers, and when we worship or share our spiritual experience through music and the sung word. Since human expressions mean something, and since not all expressions can rightly be addressed to God, Christians must be careful to parse the meanings of their expressions to determine whether they are fitting.

ARTICLE 11: On Popular Culture

We affirm that much of popular culture is formulaic and sentimentalized, and that it tends toward banality and narcissism. We affirm that much popular music, through its stereotyped form, lacks the ability to communicate transcendent truth, virtue, and beauty, which are central to worship. We further affirm that the modes of expression which have emerged from eras shaped largely by the secularizing forces of popular culture are often incompatible with ordinate affection. —∿— *We deny* that a selective rejection of popular culture is tantamount to elitism or a disdain for the average believer. We also deny that there are no contemporary examples of orthopathy, or that orthopathy can be found solely in the past.

—∿—

THE CENTRAL PREMISES of this article flow naturally from the following principles that have been developed in preceding articles:

1. Transcendent truth, goodness, and beauty are real and rooted in the nature and character of God.
2. Recognizing, affirming, and delighting in these realities is central to Christian worship.

3. One of the primary ways these realities about God are expressed is through meaningful works of the imagination.
4. These works of imagination carry more than verbal meaning, because they also foster either ordinate or inordinate affection for God.

If the foregoing are true, then it follows that some works of the imagination are ill-fitted and unworthy to express transcendent realities about God and his truth, goodness, and beauty.

Works of the imagination cannot simply be evaluated according to when they were created or who created them. The decision about what is worth using in worship cannot be based upon whether a work is "traditional" or "contemporary" as long as those terms refer simply to time. Rather, whether a work is worthy of being offered in worship must be determined by whether it has the capacity in itself to express God's values and to nurture right affection for him. In principle, every work of the imagination should be tested on this basis. In practice, however, the process of evaluation can be simplified by grouping kinds of works together on the basis of common characteristics.

One such grouping that we believe is mostly ill-fitted to Christian worship is popular culture. We believe that inherent deficiencies in the imaginative works produced by popular culture disqualify many of them from suitability for worship. As we are using the term, *popular culture* does not refer primarily either to what is new in time or to what is accessible or "popular" to ordinary people. Instead, we understand popular culture to display the following characteristics:

1. It is first of all mass culture, possible only where the means of widespread production and dissemination are available.
2. It is or quickly becomes commercial: its primary use is to make money.
3. In order to make money, it must appeal to as many people as possible.
4. It appeals to the masses by directly appealing to the appetites.
5. The direct stimulation and immediate gratification of the appetites are inherently transient.
6. This transience ensures that the consumer will never be satisfied, always returning for something more stimulating.
7. Consequently, a principal value of popular culture is novelty.

Because popular culture produces works of imagination that tend to reflect its values, they are overwhelmingly suited to consumerist, market-driven capitalism. Their ephemeral nature precludes them from reflecting the weighty, the profound, the transcendent, and the enduring. Exceptions exists, of course—but because of their transient nature, these things are powerless to reflect the permanent. Immediate gratification cannot cultivate profundity. Trivial expressions are incapable of expressing the consequential.

One final clarification: distinctions between the trivial and the consequential, or between the immediate and the enduring, are not equivalent to distinctions between complexity and simplicity. Works of the imagination can be both profound and accessible. The imaginative works produced by popular culture are not objectionable because they are accessible. They are objectionable as implements of worship because of their tendency to foster sensibilities that contradict reverent worship.

ARTICLE 12: On the Cultivation of Christian Tradition

We affirm the importance of beginning our pursuit of sound worship and holy living within the bounds of traditions that we have inherited from the saints of the entire church age (2 Tim. 2:2, Phil. 3:17). Many of these believers, even the ones with whom we would have significant theological disagreements, have had a clearer understanding of what it is to love God rightly than we do. We affirm the value of learning from the culture that developed around and in response to the growth of Christianity. ⟶ *We deny* the chronological snobbery that ignores the past, the naïve longing for some past golden age, and the postmodern inclination to isolate and select elements of historic Christian practice to suit personal taste. We further deny that Christendom represents pure and unmixed Christianity.

⟶

ONE OF THE recognizable characteristics of those Protestants who were not identified with the magisterial Reformation is a distrust of tradition. In an oft-noted irony, this has led to many churches upholding an unexamined and hardened tradition of anti-traditionalism. The New Testament, however, repeats an emphasis on the central responsibility of receiving and passing down, unaltered, the tradition. For example, Paul commended the Corinthians: "because you remember me in everything and maintain the traditions even as I delivered them to you" (1 Cor. 11:2). He also exhorted the Thessalonians, "So then, brothers, stand firm and hold to the traditions that you were taught by us, either by our spoken word or by our letter" (2 Thess. 2:15).

This respect for tradition cannot be reduced to mere doctrinal fidelity, as important as that is. Aspects of the tradition go beyond theology to practice and attitude, as in Philippians 4:9: "What you have learned and received and heard and seen in me—practice these things, and the God of peace will be with you." Christians are responsible to practice, not merely the teachings of Paul, but an entire pattern of life and piety.

Consequently, conserving Christianity entails more than conserving doctrinal propositions. The tradition is not merely doctrinal. In the context of his statement to the Corinthians, Paul's references to the tradition include the practice of head coverings and the observance of the Table, among other things.

For this reason we insist on a conservative orientation toward our discussions of worship and reverence. We would be both arrogant and unwise to discard the doctrinal tradition of the church, including all of the teachers whom God has used to develop the system of faith and to bring it to us. By the same token, we would be arrogant and unwise to resist or ignore the church's tradition of worship. Instead, when we think about worship, we will deliberately make what the church has handed down to us our starting point. We think it particularly wise to give special attention to those periods of church history in which the church has cultivated expressions of reverence and honor.

We recognize that our respect for tradition runs counter to the spirit of our age, which is consumed with the present moment. We insist that a Christianity that must change with each wind of fashion is confessing that it has nothing permanent to say. We would be immeasurably impoverished if we were forced to reinvent or even rediscover the Christian faith during each passing generation. The Christian past provides us with rich resources that we can appropriate and upon which we can build, both in our theology and in our devotion. Nothing is less relevant than a trendy church.

On the other hand, we reject two contemporary methods of appropriating the reverence and piety of past saints. One is the attempt to repristinate present-day Christianity by recovering the forms of some mythical golden age from the Christian past. We offer unqualified allegiance neither to the fathers nor to the Reformers nor to any particular age of the church. Our appropriation of any era remains critical in matters pertaining to both doctrine and affection. Nevertheless, we recognize a core of orthopathy throughout church history, as we acknowledge a core of orthodoxy.

The other is the tendency to look at past expressions of piety as a chest of curiosities out of which we may draw this or that expression to create some particular effect. We do not adopt any tradition uncritically, for we recognize that every stage of the Christian tradition includes accretions that are of merely human, and sometimes sinful, origin. Our goal is to conserve those elements of the tradition that most reflect right thinking about God, obedient conduct in the presence of God, and right love toward God.

ARTICLE 13:
On Today's Congregational Music

We affirm that twenty-first-century churches, like the churches of every age, must worship God in their own words, with their own voice. We add the qualification that these expressions must both embody ordinate affection and build on the tradition that represents it, while also answering to the twenty-first-century imagination. We further affirm that all people are to sing with understanding (1 Cor. 14:15) and that good music or poetry may be simple. Finally, we affirm that church music ought to be beautiful. —ᴡ— *We deny* that musical choices should be made to appease or attract a particular constituency in the church. We deny that the average Christian is capable of appreciating only the simplest kind of music. We deny that good music or poetry worth loving can be shallow, trivial, banal or clichéd. At the same time we also deny that Christians should worship with forms that are incomprehensible to them.

—ᴡ—

THE COMMAND to teach and admonish one another in psalms, hymns, and spiritual songs is given to all believers of every age. We are to sing to him in our day and not only using words written in the days of teh fathers. We ought to sing to him of our experience in our era, using our own words.

While the sermons of Spurgeon and Edwards are delightful and continue to bless believers, we rightly expect modern preachers to expound the Scriptures to us in their own words, using their own gifting, applying the Word to us. A church that preached only sermons from a supposed golden age of preaching would be attempting to pickle the religious experience of that time for use at every time. Preaching does not work that way, and neither does singing.

The difficulty, as we see it, has to do with the age in which we live. Just as our civilization is experiencing a general decline in the level of reading, writing, and speaking, so we are experiencing a decline in sacred music and poetry. Promising signs have appeared during the last two decades, and some of the modern hymn writers have breathed fresh air into what had become a sad repeating jukebox of gospel songs and popular choruses.

Comprehension is fundamental to worship (1 Cor. 14:15). What Protestant would object to Christians reading and worshipping in their own language? In the same way, church music ought to be enjoyable and palatable for the ordinary

71

Christian. The problem is that the general decline of discernment regarding beauty and form has led churchgoers to confound the accessibility of hymns with their value as popular entertainments. Nevertheless, all Christians, regardless of education or background, are capable of apprehending beauty and experiencing the transcendent. Beauty is comprehensible to all, but not everything that is familiar or easily recognizable is beautiful. On the other hand, not everything that is beautiful will be grasped easily or become familiar quickly by the average musical palate.

Because popular music has become sonic wallpaper, people are most familiar with its predictable, formulaic, and clichéd musical tricks. These are usually shallow, trivial, and incapable of carrying the weight of worship or expressing the depth and range of feeling that belongs to Christian piety. Simply because people find these expressions familiar and accessible does not mean that they should be most readily used. Rather, present-day composers need to hold the genuine Christian tradition with one hand and the twenty-first-century imagination with the other, seeking to compose in our day a kind of hymnody that will teach the church how to worship God ordinately. We see some indications—perhaps a cloud the size of a man's hand—of the beginnings of some useful, serious, hymnody that will employ the idioms of our day to evoke affections fitting of our God.

ARTICLE 14: On Our Children

We affirm the necessity of passing these values to our children through regular catechesis, in faithful family worship, and by welcoming all ages into the corporate worship of our churches (Deut. 6:7, Eph. 6:4). Children learn rightly ordered worship and have their imaginations and affections appropriately shaped largely through observation and participation. Thus churches should encourage families to worship together in the corporate gatherings of the church as much as possible or practical. —⁓— *We deny* that the family is more important than or replaces a local church. We further deny that we can adopt a model of children's ministry which aims to entertain our children and still expect them to learn the grace of meaningful worship.

—⁓—

He did much towards the instruction
of his children in the way of familiar discourse . . .
which made them love home, and delight in his company,
and greatly endeared religion to them.
—Matthew Henry, speaking of his father Philip

In their book *Classical Education,* Gene Veith and Andrew Kern observe, "Classical education turns on the vision of what man is, of his responsibilities, and of the curriculum and method that follow from this vision." For our purposes, we could drop the word *classical.* All education turns on the vision of the nature and purpose of humanity.

We reject the Enlightenment vision of humans as fundamentally *homo sapiens,* although they certainly are that. More importantly, we believe that humans are *homo adorans,* created to love and worship God. Humans are who they are because they were created in God's image, after God's likeness, and their fundamental nature corresponds to their fundamental responsibility—to love the Lord with all their heart, soul, mind, and strength. Without love, everything else is nothing.

When it comes to making disciples of our children in our churches, pure love is what we are after. This love is not a mindless "emotion," as is clear from our commitment to thorough, biblical, catechetical instruction. But this love cannot be confined to robust doctrine. We will not pass on the faith whole and entire simply by passing on propositions, however necessary propositions may be. We must model for our children a kind of loyal trust in God that draws their affections to the simple but substantial gifts of grace by which the Lord communicates his love to us. We want their affections to be devoted to the apostles' teaching and to fellowship, to the breaking of bread, and to the prayers.

Consequently, we oppose all the anthropocentric, progressivist reforms that have dominated educational philosophy and practice during the past century. These putative reforms can only produce "men without chests," as C. S. Lewis put it. We resist an overly rationalistic conception of the human person which reduces "getting something" out of the church service to a question of whether a five year old can trace the argument of a fifty minute expository sermon. The very fact that we ask the question in that way reflects poorly upon our knowledge of ourselves and our knowledge of worship. G. K. Chesterton once said, "It would be too high and hopeful a compliment to say that the world is becoming absolutely babyish. For its chief weak-mindedness is an inability to appreciate the intelligence of babies."

We celebrate the intellectual quickness and stunning spiritual capacity of children, but we also take seriously the fact that they arrive with disordered affections. Foolishness is bound in their hearts, and it would be cruel to feed their appetites rather than to give them the remedy. Proverbs 1:7 says, "The fear of the Lord is the beginning of wisdom; fools despise wisdom and instruction." Though children will naturally despise the wisdom of godly worship, learning to humbly receive the Lord's good gifts of grace is the beginning of a lifetime of coming to know the Lord. We want boys who learn to worship like virtuous men from their sober, strong, and kind fathers—not from Squeaky the clown or Mr. Sports Celebrity.

We want girls who learn to worship like excellent women from their loyal, spirited, and perceptive mothers—not from a cheerleader or Miss Imitation American Idol.

Proverbs 1:7 is perhaps the single most potent educational principle in Scripture. We might also observe both in Proverbs, and in the entire canon, that father and mother are the most significant force for the instruction of their children. We believe that church and parents should work together to harness this power, partly by encouraging families to worship together.

The attentive reader should note that this article does not prescribe any rigid methodology for training children, nor does it necessarily proscribe methodologies like camps or youth groups. It certainly does not invite families to take the place of the church in their children's lives. It also recognizes the existence of special situations, for example, the needs of infants or the presence of children from unchurched families. We are simply pleading for churches to recognize the crucial place of the affections in the discipleship of our children, as well as the central role that the family and the gathered congregation play in that formation.

I love the Word of God. I esteem it above all.
I find my heart so inclined. I desire it as the food of my soul.
I greatly delight in it, both in reading and hearing of it. . . .
I love the ministers and the messengers of the Word.
—Matthew Henry, age 11

Article 15: On Local Churches and the Sovereignty of God

We affirm the primacy of the local church in the conservation and nourishment of historic, biblical Christianity. We affirm that godly elders must patiently teach God's Word and model right belief, living, and loving (1 Tim. 3:15, 4:16). We further affirm that such efforts must be fully dependent upon the sovereign will of God, which will ultimately be accomplished (Dan. 4:34–35). —⁓— *We deny* that the transmission of the Christian faith will occur primarily by individuals alone, in families disconnected from local churches, or through parachurch ministries. We further deny that the preservation of Christianity is ultimately dependent upon the meager efforts of finite people and especially any pragmatic methodology or programs.

—⁓—

IN THIS DECLARATION, we have outlined a call to know the Lord in the full dimensions of his truth, beauty, and goodness. But where will the world full of error, ugliness, and evil see such glory made known?

Jesus has already outlined his plan to manifest his glory in the world today. He said, "I will build my church" (Matt. 16:18).

Jesus Christ died and rose again to save his people from their sins, and as the Spirit applies his work in the world, a newly created body is growing up into Christ. That church is manifested in local assemblies around the world, and these on-the-ground communities provide the life context for making disciples.

Jesus has equipped these churches with just what is needed to nourish and conserve historic, biblical Christianity. Pastors and teachers preach and teach the Word, equipping the members of the body to build one another up to maturity. To each member is given the manifestation of the Spirit for the common good. In these actual, gathered communities, God's people can learn by experience what is excellent. Of course, if these assemblies pass on banal, trite, slipshod Christianity, the damage is very great. No parachurch ministry can make up the difference.

One of the reasons that no other kind of ministry can make up the difference is because Jesus has given these actual, gathered communities genuine authority (Matt. 18:15–22). To them Jesus has committed the administration of baptism and the Lord's Supper. A podcast preacher or a writing teacher may do any number of good things for the saints, but these things always fall short of full-orbed Christianity. At the heart of Christianity is the church. No other institution or human organization on the earth today can do what the church does. No wonder God says that the church is the pillar and support of the truth. Actually, the gathered churches must hold this glory high.

The final affirmation of this document is not simply a tag line, a generic affirmation that God will ultimately do what he wants to do. It is rather a substantive assertion of a basic principle of conservatism, which serves a two-fold purpose.

Positively, it grounds our hope in God and lifts our eyes to his grand plan of redemption. Conservatives are known for pursuing the permanent things. What can be more permanent than the glorious, universal reign of the Alpha and Omega?

Negatively, it keeps placing our trust in any methodological fix. We are sometimes presented with selective statistics, bereft of biblical backing, and then told that we "must" do ministry a certain way. When this occurs, we cringe at the arrogance of puny minds which refuse to submit to the work of the Spirit. When we are sold the latest ministry paradigm which (we are told) is sure to produce results, we decline to pay even pocket change for it.

As you consider this declaration, we ask you to do so with the spirit expressed by Hosea's words, "Let us know; let us press on to know the Lord." We want to behold the Lord's glory, in all of his truth, goodness, and beauty, and we ask you to join us in this noble quest. May he receive glory in the church and in Christ Jesus throughout all generations, forever and ever. Amen.

Appendix A:
The Apostles' Creed

The Apostles' Creed appeared as early as 390 and is widely believed to be based upon beliefs articulated by the twelve apostles.

I believe in God,
    the Father almighty,
    Creator of heaven and earth,
and in Jesus Christ, his only Son, our Lord,
    who was conceived by the Holy Spirit,
    born of the Virgin Mary,
    suffered under Pontius Pilate,
    was crucified, died and was buried;
    he descended into hell;
    on the third day he rose again from the dead;
    he ascended into heaven,
    and is seated at the right hand of God the Father almighty;
    from there he will come to judge the living and the dead.
I believe in the Holy Spirit,
    the holy catholic Church,
    the communion of saints,
    the forgiveness of sins,
    the resurrection of the body,
        and life everlasting. Amen.

Appendix B: The Nicene Creed

The Nicene Creed was adopted by the church council that met in Nicaea in 325 and was revised by the Council of Constantinople in 381.

WE BELIEVE in one God,
the Father, the Almighty,
    maker of heaven and earth,
    of all that is, seen and unseen.

WE BELIEVE in one Lord, Jesus Christ,
the only Son of God,
    eternally begotten of the Father,
    God from God, Light from Light,
    true God from true God,
    begotten, not made,
    of one Being with the Father.
    Through him all things were made.
    For us and for our salvation
        he came down from heaven:
by the power of the Holy Spirit
he became incarnate from the Virgin Mary,
    and was made man.

For our sake he was crucified under Pontius Pilate;
    he suffered death and was buried.
    On the third day he rose again
in accordance with the Scriptures;
    he ascended into heaven
        and is seated at the right hand of the Father.
He will come again in glory to judge the living and the dead,
    and his kingdom will have no end.

WE BELIEVE in the Holy Spirit, the Lord, the giver of life,
who proceeds from the Father and the Son.
    With the Father and the Son he is worshiped and glorified.
    He has spoken through the Prophets.

WE BELIEVE in one holy catholic and apostolic Church.
    We acknowledge one baptism for the forgiveness of sins.
    We look for the resurrection of the dead,
        and the life of the world to come. Amen.

Appendix C:
The Definition of Chalcedon

This statement was adopted at the Council of Chalcedon in 451.

WE, THEN, following the holy Fathers, all with one consent, teach men to confess one and the same Son, our Lord Jesus Christ, the same perfect in Godhead and also perfect in manhood; truly God and truly man, of a reasonable [rational] soul and body; consubstantial [co-essential] with the Father according to the Godhead, and consubstantial with us according to the Manhood; in all things like unto us, without sin; begotten before all ages of the Father according to the Godhead, and in these latter days, for us and for our salvation, born of the Virgin Mary, the Mother of God, according to the Manhood; one and the same Christ, Son, Lord, only begotten, to be acknowledged in two natures, inconfusedly, unchangeably, indivisibly, inseparably; the distinction of natures being by no means taken away by the union, but rather the property of each nature being preserved, and concurring in one Person and one Subsistence, not parted or divided into two persons, but one and the same Son, and only begotten, God the Word, the Lord Jesus Christ; as the prophets from the beginning [have declared] concerning him, and the Lord Jesus Christ Himself has taught us, and the Creed of the holy Fathers has handed down to us.

Appendix D:
The Athanasian Creed

The Athanasian Creed is a fifth–sixth-century confession.

WHOSOEVER WILL BE SAVED, before all things it is necessary that he hold the catholic faith. Which faith except every one do keep whole and undefiled; without doubt he shall perish everlastingly. And the catholic faith is this: That we worship one God in Trinity, and Trinity in Unity; Neither confounding the Persons; nor dividing the Essence. For there is one Person of the Father; another of the Son; and another of the Holy Ghost. But the Godhead of the Father, of the Son, and of the Holy Ghost, is all one; the Glory equal, the Majesty coeternal. Such as the Father is; such is the Son; and such is the Holy Ghost. The Father uncreated; the Son uncreated; and the Holy Ghost uncreated. The Father unlimited; the Son unlimited; and the Holy Ghost unlimited. The Father eternal; the Son eternal; and the Holy Ghost eternal. And yet they are not three eternals; but one eternal. As also there are not three uncreated; nor three infinites, but one uncreated; and one infinite. So likewise the Father is Almighty; the Son Almighty; and the Holy Ghost Almighty. And yet they are not three Almighties; but one Almighty. So the Father is God; the Son is God; and the Holy Ghost is God. And yet they are not three Gods; but one God. So likewise the Father is Lord; the Son Lord; and the Holy Ghost Lord. And yet not three Lords; but one Lord. For like as we are compelled by the Christian verity; to acknowledge every Person by himself to be God and Lord; So are we forbidden by the catholic religion; to say, There are three Gods, or three Lords. The Father is made of none; neither created, nor begotten. The Son is of the Father alone; not made, nor created; but begotten. The Holy Ghost is of the Father and of the Son; neither made, nor created, nor begotten; but proceeding. So there is one Father, not three Fathers; one Son, not three Sons; one Holy Ghost, not three Holy Ghosts. And in this Trinity none is before, or after another; none is greater, or less than another. But the whole three Persons are coeternal, and coequal. So that in all things, as aforesaid; the Unity in Trinity, and the Trinity in Unity, is to be worshipped. He therefore that will be saved, let him thus think of the Trinity.

Furthermore it is necessary to everlasting salvation; that he also believe faithfully the Incarnation of our Lord Jesus Christ. For the right Faith is, that we believe and confess; that our Lord Jesus Christ, the Son of God, is God and Man; God, of the Essence of the Father; begotten before the worlds; and Man, of the Essence of his Mother, born in the world. Perfect God; and perfect Man, of a reasonable soul and human flesh subsisting. Equal to the Father, as touching his Godhead; and inferior to the Father as touching his Manhood. Who although he is God and Man; yet he is not two, but one Christ. One; not by conversion of the Godhead into flesh; but by assumption of the Manhood by God. One altogether; not by confusion of Essence; but by unity of Person. For as the reasonable soul and flesh is one man; so God and Man is one Christ; Who suffered for our salvation; descended into hell; rose again the third day from the dead. He ascended into heaven, he sitteth on the right hand of the God the Father Almighty, from whence he will come to judge the living and the dead. At whose coming all men will rise again with their bodies; And shall give account for their own works. And they that have done good shall go into life everlasting; and they that have done evil, into everlasting fire. This is the catholic faith; which except a man believe truly and firmly, he cannot be saved.

Appendix E:
Post-Reformation Confessions

The following web sites contain the full text of post-Reformation confessions, agreement with at least one of which (or confessions with similar doctrinal particulars) we believe is necessary for defining biblical Christianity.

The Belgic Confession of Faith

This Dutch Reformed confession authored in 1567 is a confessional standard to which many Reformed churches subscribe. You can read the text of this confession at: https://www.rca.org/sslpage.aspx?pid=317.

The Schleitheim Confession

Swiss Anabaptists in Schleitheim adopted this confession in 1527. You can read the text of this confession at: http://www.anabaptists.org/history/the-schleitheim-confession.html.

The Westminster Confession of Faith

Composed by the 1646 Westminster Assembly to be a confession of the Church of England, this confession has been adopted by many Presbyterian and other Reformed groups and served as a model for the Second London Baptist

Confession. You can read the text of this confession at: http://www.pcaac.org/resources/wcf.

The Second London Baptist Confession / The Philadelphia Baptist Confession

Many Reformed Baptists subscribe to this 1689 confession penned by Particular Baptists in England and modeled after the Westminster Confession of Faith. The confession was adopted by the Philadelphia Association of Baptist Churches in 1707. You can read the text of this confession at: http://www.reformed.org/documents/index.html? mainframe=whttp://www.reformed.org/documents/ baptist_1689.html.

The Thirty-Nine Articles of the Church of England

This document established the doctrinal core for the Church of England beginning in 1563. You can read the text of this confession at: http://www.thirtyninearticles.org.

The New Hampshire Baptist Confession

Penned as a confession of faith for the New Hampshire Baptist Convention in 1833, this document is widely adopted by Baptists in America. You can read the text of this confession at: http://www.ccel.org/ccel/schaff/creeds3.v.ii.ii.html.

The Baptist Faith and Message

This statement of faith of the Southern Baptist Convention was originally written in 1925 and has been revised on three subsequent occasions. You can read the 2000 revision at: http://www.sbc.net/bfm2000/bfm2000.asp.

COLOPHON —⁓—

A CONSERVATIVE CHRISTIAN DECLARATION was set in 12-point Arno, a 2007 typeface designed by Robert Slimbach, who created a contemporary version based on classic Venitian forms. Named for the river that flows through Florence, Italy, Arno is a typeface adopted by designers who are comfortable working within artistic boundaries. The interior design reflects a long tradition of beautifully blocked pages with generous spacing and margins—a book to be read and cherished, not a reference work to sit on the shelf. The design is *conservative* in the sense that it projects a timeless quality, reminding readers of a volume set in hot metal, subtly suggesting that the book (and its premise) has always existed.

18383503R00056

Made in the USA
San Bernardino, CA
12 January 2015